Drawing with Shapes Is Fun!

DRAWING A BUTTERFLY WITH CIRCLES

BREE PAVONE

PowerKiDS press.

New York

Published in 2019 by The Rosen Publishing Group, Inc.
29 East 21st Street, New York, NY 10010

Revised Edition, 2019

Editor: Greg Roza
Book Design: Reann Nye

Photo Credits: Cover, 1–22 (background) piotr_pabijan/Shutterstock.com; cover, 1–22 (markers) Photo Melon/Shutterstock.com; pp. 5, 24 Lightspring/Shutterstock.com.

Cataloging-in-Publication Data

Names: Pavone, Bree.
Title: Drawing a butterfly with circles / Bree Pavone.
Description: New York : PowerKids Press, 2019. | Series: Drawing with shapes is fun! | Includes index.
Identifiers: LCCN ISBN 9781538331163 (pbk.) | ISBN 9781538331156 (library bound) | ISBN 9781538331170 (6 pack)
Subjects: LCSH: Butterflies in art–Juvenile literature. | Circle in art–Juvenile literature. | Drawing–Technique–Juvenile literature.
Classification: LCC NC655.P38 2019 | DDC 743.6'5789–dc23

Manufactured in the United States of America

CPSIA Compliance Information: Batch #CS18PK: For Further Information contact Rosen Publishing, New York, New York at 1-800-237-9932

CONTENTS

Butterflies use their **wings** to fly.
Let's draw a butterfly!

5

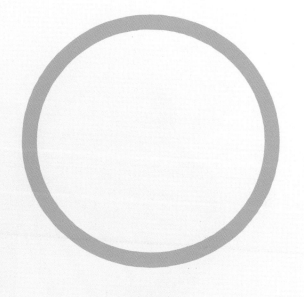

6

Draw a green circle to make part of a wing for your butterfly.

Draw a blue circle to make part of the next wing for your butterfly.

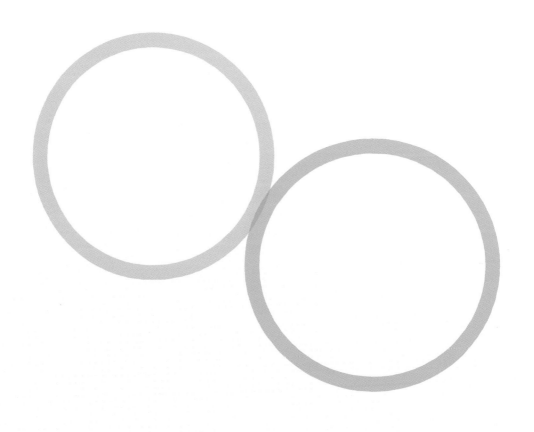

9

10

Draw a small pink circle on the right wing of your butterfly.

Draw a small yellow circle on the left wing of your butterfly.

13

14

Draw two small orange circles on the top wings of your butterfly.

Draw two small red circles on the bottom wings.

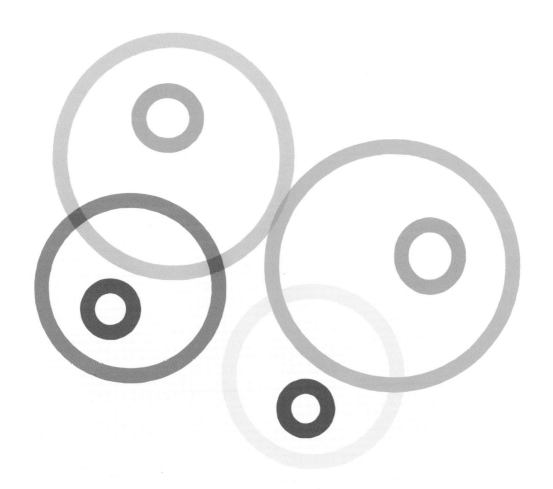

17

18

Draw a small black circle for the **head** of your butterfly.

Draw seven smaller purple circles for the **body** of your butterfly.

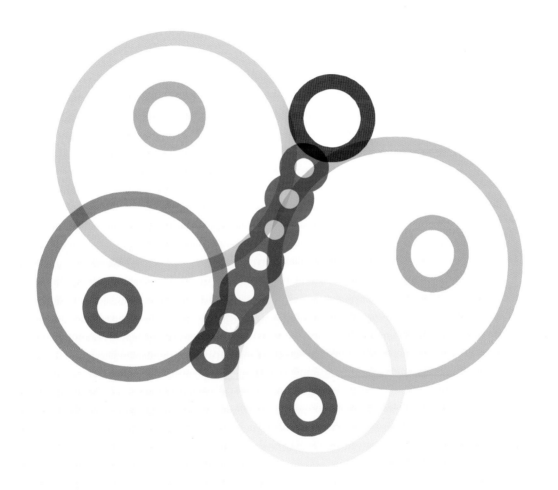

21

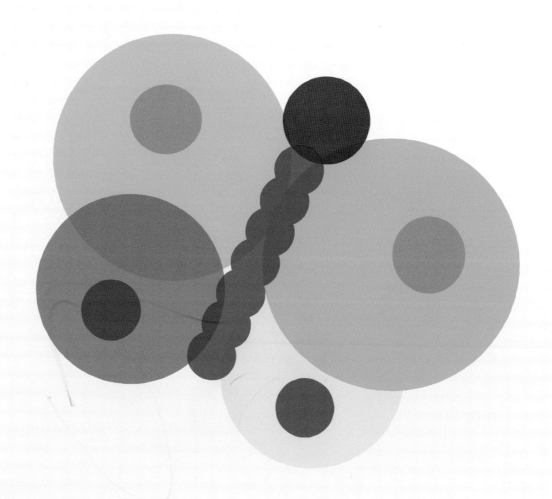

22

Color in your butterfly. Nice work!

23

WORDS TO KNOW

body

head

wing

INDEX

WEBSITES

Due to the changing nature of Internet links, PowerKids Press has developed an online list of websites related to the subject of this book. This site is updated regularly. Please use this link to access the list: www.powerkidslinks.com/dws/bfly